SEASONS OF CHANGE

A COLLECTION OF POETRY

ERNEST ROBERSON, SR

Seasons of Change

A Collection of Poetry

Ernest Roberson, Sr.

Copyright © 2021 by Trient Press

All rights reserved. No part of this publication may be reproduced, distributed, or transmitted in any form or by any means, including photocopying, recording, or other electronic or mechanical methods, without the prior written permission of the publisher, except in the case of brief quotations embodied in critical reviews and certain other noncommercial uses permitted by copyright law. For permission requests, write to the publisher, addressed "Attention: Permissions Coordinator," at the address below.

Criminal copyright infringement, including infringement without monetary gain, is investigated by the FBI and is punishable by up to five years in federal prison and a fine of $250,000.

Except for the original story material written by the author, all songs, song titles, and lyrics mentioned in the novel The Silent Wars are the exclusive property of the respective artists, songwriters, and copyright holder.

Trient Press
3375 S Rainbow Blvd
#81710, SMB 13135
Las Vegas,NV 89180

Ordering Information:
Quantity sales. Special discounts are available on quantity purchases by corporations, associations, and others. For details, contact the publisher at the address above.
Orders by U.S. trade bookstores and wholesalers. Please contact Trient Press: Tel: (775) 996-3844; or visit www.trientpress.com.

Printed in the United States of America

Publisher's Cataloging-in-Publication data
Roberson, Sr. , Ernest
A title of a book :Seasons of Change

ISBN Hardcover : 978-1-955198-11-0
    Paperback : 978-1-955198-17-2
    E-book   : 978-1-955198-18-9

DEDICATION

This book is in Remembrance of Zachary Monroe Sarvis, resting in Peace since 1990 and dearly missed.

"Your Presence I Miss,

Your Memory I Treasure,

Loving You Always,

Forgetting You Never. "

For my three loving children, Jersey Lynn, Ernest Jr and Aaron Columbus, who shine on.

A word is dead when it's said, some say.

I say it just begins to live, that day.

    E.R.SR.

PART ONE
LOVE

For My Love

With your tears running down,
Why do you always frown?
Is it because she left you one day?
Is it because she could not stay, because
    of my ways?
On my branches you would swing and smile.
Do you still long for the happiness
    that you know I can give you?
You found shade under my body that
    will never fade.
Stop your fears, I can and will do something
    to stop your tears.
I know you think I want change, but I know
    I will.
Whatever happens, I will always remember you.
And I know I will always be in your
    heart.
I had it all at one time, but I lost it.
I never want to lose it again.
If I change my ways, I know I'll have
    more days to love you.

If one thing I know, I know I love you
    and I want to be with you.
Just remember, I'll always love you.
If you believe me, and believe this is true.
Just tell me how much you love me.

Somebody Special

From every housetop,
I'd like to shout it,
    and don't you doubt it.
If I were a sky writer,
    I'd write in the sky,
"I know who loves you, how much
    and why."
I'd whisper in your ear,
    a love song overdue.
You're someone special.
Because someone loves you.
If you should ask of me,
    of those who love you best.
I'd say, "I'm that someone."

Thoughts

If the stars would shine in the heavens
    Tonight,
Casting shadows on our souls,
And whippoorwills would sing their songs,
As a dove softly coos,
And the star lit sky played your mind,
Like imagery of a dream,
Would your thoughts be taken for just one
    moment
To see that I love you?
Imagine that I had all the riches to behold.
Within the love of my heart.
And all the trails and famines that ever
    existed.
Could not pull us apart.

Imagine the lines of the most beautiful
    poems.
Fairy tales of love so true.

All are of happy endings.
Just as my love for you.
What if the stars did shine in the heavens
    tonight?
Would I be there with you?
And would you believe and trust in me
When I say, "I love you"?

Shadows of Your Memory

Shadows of your memory.

Will never die in my heart.

Just as the miles between us.

Doesn't seem that far apart.

It's the love I have for you, soft and blue.

A dream isn't a dream, if without you.

Yet it's only in my mind.

Shadows of your memory

Keeps me from being free.

When I'm out with someone.

It's you that I see.

I can't help this feeling, deep inside.

The longing to hold you, in my eyes.

I'm loving you, in my mind.

Shadows of your memory.

Your pictures on my wall.

Every day I see myself.

Just about to fall.

It's the way I see you, in my arms.

As gentle as a clear night, full of stars.

But I have you, only in my mind.

Believe

For now, I stand aside in your life.
For we know why, and what we believe in.
Others will deceive.
But remember when you awake each morning
    be sure to plan your day
To only do good things all through, and from that
    do not stray.
For you and I there is no limit.
And knowledge is our key.
We feel like we're in a trap of senseless lies.
But is this pain, and sorrow only in our minds?
We share a secret,
But why must we keep it hide?
Why do we feel so blank?
So misunderstood?
People will deceive me, but I remain a believer.

We feel so enmeshed by our frowns.
For we both knew that we can't live a decent life,
    of truth and honesty.

For it the truth wasn't blind,
They still wouldn't find it acceptable with peaceful
    minds.
But for now, others hearing of our secret would argue.
I want quit believing, in things that I believe
    in.
For truth is truth.
As love is love.
If they found out our secret, don't agree to cease
    to exist.
Reality is you and me.
And in time the deceivers will believe as we have
    of our secret.

In a slack society, proceeding to decay.
There's many of answers to enfold.
For me there's no faintest need to shirk.
In a time, I'm being deceived.
But strong I am, to remain a believer.
The world may see us wrong.
And grey clouds try to hide our sun.
Our tears, and the rain commingle.

And our lives seem no longer fun.

    For they try to deceive, our beliefs.

Lovers at First Sight

I've lost loved ones in my life.
So I've seen my share of pain.
And a few days ago, I left a piece of love
    behind.
Couldn't take the pain any longer.
Oh, my love.
A piece of love, that another was
    loving,
Now there's one thing you should know.
I've been lost and lonely.
But let me tell you this.
Love has its mysteries.
And you can't explain just how it begins.
It's not hard for me to see the light,
That we were meant to be.

I'll hold you in my arms every day and
    night.
And tell you all the things that I really
    feel.

Oh, my love, I'll show you that my love is
      real.
One glance was all it took and I
      knew.
I only wanted to love you.
And holding you would make things
      okay.
Oh, my love.
Lover's at first sight.
Just when I thought I had all the answers.
One glance was all it took and I
      knew.

You and I were just so right.
Oh, my love.
Lovers at first sight.
All I need to complete my life is you.
Oh, my love.
Lovers at first sight.
I was looking for someone to love and
      understand me.
Oh, my love.

You are the best thing in my life.

All This Time

There's been times when it seemed that I was so
    alone.
And there's been times when it seemed that
    all my troubles had no end.
And it seems that I've faced this world
    with no one by my side.
And this heart of mine has loved,
    to only be broken in the end.
And it seemed that at times I had this world
    strapped against my back.
I know that time was what I needed,
    for my heart to mend.

Never did I know that you'd be the one
    to come into my life
And mend this heart of mine.
You told me of a love that's true
And not hard to define.
So I guess that I was blind.

For I didn't see you standing there all that
> time.
No, I can't believe it.
Nor did I see it.
But I feel what I've been missing, all of this
> time.
Now I face this world no longer alone.
And it seems like my heart is feeling love
> for the first time.
And here's something easy to define for yourself.
You're my best friend and lover
> until the end of time.

Hear the Kind Echoes

As I look back over the years,
    back when our eyes first met,
And our feelings were unexplainable within ourselves
    for one another.
Nothing seemed to be the limit.
Hand and hand across those years,
    faults were thin, while love was thick.
Now as I sit here remembering,
I see why memories are made,
    made not to be forgotten.
You showed me how love should feel,
And that there is someone up above.
You helped me find the things that I have
    missed.
And feelings I never knew laid within
    me.
As I speak of you, these words,
Hopefully you'll always hear
    hear the kind echoes.

I Found Love (When I Found You)

Another morning finds me.
I know the sun will shine.
Now and then I stumble,
But your love helps me forget.
I breathe your name with every breath
And I'm finding that the longer I'm with you
The deeper in love I fall.
Because you make it so easy to love you,
Though now and then I stumble.
I never forget how much you mean to me.
No matter if my head is bowed low.
You're the angel which is on my mind.

Another morning finds me.
And I've got your sweet love on my mind.
You're always a lady,
And never too far away.
Once I held your sweet love
And felt your tender touch.

I found that the longer I'm with you,
The deeper in love I fall.
> Just because you make it so easy to love you.

From the First Moment

From the moment that I laid my eyes on you,
I knew it was true love.
And I had fallen for you.
From the first moment you held me in your arms,
I felt you.
I felt your love that you had for me
     deep inside.
From the first moment that you kissed me,
I knew that you loved me.
And when you looked into my eyes,
I felt your love deep inside.
For the first time, I am aware of what might happen.
For I want to be yours, and yours alone.
Until my last breath I take.

They Don't Say Goodbye

Through all those complex years
She thought she was alone.
And never did she care to look around,
    to see that the memories still remained.
Maybe she should've cried at times,
And spared herself some pain.
But she's been chasing her dreams,
And no one ever heard her when she called.
In her eyes you can see the sorrow of all those
    complex years.
And the worries of her tomorrow.
But she'll still be chasing her dreams,
Feeling like a prisoner of his life.
Chained, shackled, and judged by his ways.
Some would say he's a loser, for he seldom got
    things right.

But she appeared like a dream to him.
And he knew from that moment he laid eyes

on her,
He had fallen for her, and he had to let her
> know.
So he said: I'd give my heart and soul, if you'll
> show me the light to yours.
And I'll keep you near to my heart, if you'll love me
> forever.
And I'd do anything to try and make you happy.
Though some things I can't give, you'll always have my heart.
And for the first time in her life,
She no longer lived in a world of her own.
And she felt love deep inside.
And finally seen forever in her heart
> for them.

Through all of her complex years.
And feeling like a prisoner of his life.
For life's about change, and they don't say good-bye.
> No, they don't say good-bye.

The Letter

You may find it odd that I'm writing you a letter,
Now that I'm with you more.
But sometimes we as humans don't express ourselves enough.
Then a day comes when we wished that we had, have said more,
Even though you knew it all along.
I've never felt any better in my life.
And now I see why people has always said that changes are good.
I took a chance, and never regretted it ever since.
I'm happy, and for the first time, I a long time
I've loved, cared about, and understand.
Never did I ever think that I'd be where I am today.
Nor did I think that I'd truthfully love, and care about someone,
After all the hunt that I've been through.
And all this time I thought that I had all the answers.
But I didn't.
You're my purpose in life, and the best thing that's
Ever happened to me.
With love, trust, and faith.
I love you, and I'll always love you.

Eternal

Every day filled with dreams.
Bright, new, brand new hopeful schemes.
Large shades and a great big blue sky.
First light of loving in your eyes soon to dim.
And then you flee,
Leaving me alone with me.
The things I fear, the things you said.
Burning rivers are still in my head.
Think of all we shared.
My soul so old, so young, so bare.
Afraid of you, of life.
Afraid of you not being my wife.
Until the bright new dreams began again.
The landscape never quite the same,
Eventually a different game.
Aware at last of what I know, and think,
    and am, and feel.
The gift of love is eternal for you and me.

Amazing Love

My face displays loneliness,

As my heart gazes of truth affirming.

And I find within the memories, remain

For an amazing love.

I cannot see why you feel like giving it all up.

Is easy to say

But not so easy to do.

Every day someone is giving it all up.

Mirrored here my life tells a story

For an amazing love

All my days.

All my life.

Amazing love shined on me in the midst of my darkest times.

Your love shined just for me.

And you made a way when there seemed to be no way at all.

All of you love which rained down on me.

Has given me strength, for another day.

I just have to say that……

You are my amazing love, forevermore.

My Glory Is You

There were times that I reached forward, to what lied ahead.
Though it's been hard for me to forget, what lied behind me.
Then you come along and helped me to see
What more could be ahead.
As I forgot what lied behind me.
Though it took some time.
And within that time, you had tears to fall, from my eyes.
But here you are, still by my side,
Never breaking the ties between you and me.
Now I see that my glory is you.
And nothing tells more about me than what others see in you.
And when they consider the countenance of you,
      They'll see everything that I've invested and withhold.
But they'll see what kind of character I have, also.
But within that time, you had tears to fall from your eyes.
And here you are, still by my side,
Never breaking the ties between you and me.
So, baby, thanks for hanging in there
And for getting my attention, for you've marked my life.
Now that I see that my glory is you,

As I reach forward to what lies ahead and
Forget what lies behind me.

Time is on our side,
Though it took you quite a while to while
To hold my hand.
But I was patient,
For it was all in the plan.
Though it's a mystery, you took a chance.
It's in the hands of fate
If we'll make it,
Until were sure about it.
But you never know.
It's hard to say sometimes
Where a love will lead.
So, dry your eyes
And wet your lips by kissing mine.

The Love Letter

Dear Sweetheart,

As I sat down to write this,

I thought of all you are to me.

Since the day we first met,

I wouldn't change anything about you.

I love you just the way you are.

I'm so glad that you are mine.

You're more than I ever hoped for-better than gold and rubies

Every time I think about you, I thank god for you.

You bring such joy to my life that is makes my heart sing.

I want my love to be the same to you.

When you are afraid, I will quiet your fears.

When you are depressed or discouraged,

I want to hold you and give you strength.

I am here to help you.

I would not only climb the highest mountain for you,

But I would level the mountains before you.

When I'm alone with you,

                                                Love,

                                                Your knight in shining armor.

Love of My Life

I knew you faced the hardest times,
And many times your eyes
Fought back the tears,
As your youthful would was about to fall in
And your slender shoulders
Bore the weight of all your fears.
So I'll give your heart time to heal,
And when you're ready, I'll be there.
As I see the time hands.
They're ticking' by me every day,
Falling in love.
You know I'm not much on words,
But I got to tell you how I feel.
So open your eyes, don't try to hide my love,
Because you're the only one for me.
The thought of you
Picks me up when I'm lonely.
True love, and joy, and faith.
All my strength I give to you.
My love is your exclusively

To enjoy and raise as you want to.
For you have turned into a prayer.
So free your mind for the journey.
I knew you were the perfect girl.
But for you, I thank the stars in the
Heaven above.
Love of my life.

The Plan

Time is on our side,

Though it took you quite a while to wait,

To hold my hand,

For it was all in the plan.

Though it's a mystery, you took a chance.

It's in the hands of fate

If we'll make it.

But you never know.

It's hard to say sometimes

Where a love will lead.

So, dry your eyes

And wet your lips by kissing mine.

Realize

If I could, I'd write for you a rainbow

And splash it with all the colors of God,

And hang it in the window of your being.

So that each new God's morning

Your eyes would open first.

To hope and promise.

If I could, I'd wipe away your tears

And hold you close forever in shalom.

But God never promised I could write a rainbow,

Never promised I could suffer for you,

Only promised I could love you.

That I do.

Valentine's Day

I have searched my heart
For the words to say
Just how much you mean to me
This Valentine's Day.
You are all of God's blessings
Rolled into one.
My dreams, my desires,
My nightfall, my sun,
My every waking moment,
My hopes and my fears,
My disillusion, my contentment,
My joy and my tears.
But most important of all,
I thank God when I pray.
Because you make every moment
My Valentine's Day.

Most of All

I love being with you.
I love all the joy that having you in my life
Bring me.
From our most intimate moments alone
To the pride I feel in you.
When we're out somewhere together.
I love all that we share.
I love the laughter, the understanding,
And the fact that so much about us,
Our minds, our bodies, our hearts, out feelings,
Should touch so closely and perfectly.
Together….
Most of all,
I love you
And the special, gentle way you have,
That sensitive and loving side of you,
That you save just for me when we're alone.
Together.

You're an Angel

You're an angel
That I used to kiss, every morning.
Then I'd rush home to love you,
As we felt that there was nothing
When we were together that we couldn't do.
You've put colors in my life,
And stood by, and behind me.
You're the closest thing to Heaven
That I'll ever know.
For you're an angel
That flew to close to the ground.
And as the years passed us by,
I knew that God was missing an angel.
Now things have been taken for granted,
And our hearts broke in two.
My promise I couldn't keep,
So now I'm finding it hard to even sleep.
And the colors have seemed to fade,
Day after day,
To black, and gray.

But I hope that someday
God will let me hold His angel
Once more,
As I pray, that we won't stray.

A Photograph of You

When the evening shadows gather,
After all my work is through,
I can't keep my eyes from straying
To a photograph of you.
There it rests upon my table
Just the way you looked that day,
When I first heard you say
Words of love that made me happy
And made all my dreams come true.
But-tonight, I'm all alone with
Just a photograph of you.
For one day our country called you
And you so bravely said "here."
Oh, I'm proud of you, my solider,
Yet I brush away a tear
Because I miss your cheery whistle,
Miss your footsteps on the floor,
Miss your strong arms and your kisses
That can banish all my fears.
Then I wonder if you're lonely.
Yes, I know you miss me, too,

While I sit here dreaming, gazing
At that photograph of you.
So I tiptoe to my window,
Kneel and wish upon a star,
As I pray to God to keep you safe,
No matter where you are.
Thus, my heart is ever with you
While I wait the long days through,
And the dearest of all my treasures
Is that photograph of you.
When the years have told their story
And the world is once more free,
I'll be waiting for you, darling.
There will still be you and me,
Then we'll build our dreams together,
Hand in hand, the long years through.
But forever in my heart I'll hold
That photograph of you.

Our Youngest Child

You were a tiny blessing
We could not wait to meet.
A miracle from God above,
To make our family complete.
And oh, how you were pampered
And spoiled right from the start.
As the youngest of the family,
Loved with all our hearts
And every day, dear youngest,
From the dawn to setting sun,
We've considered you a special gift,
And counted memories one by one.
We have cherished every moment,
And we wanted you to know
You have brought real joy into our lives,
And we love you so.

Our First Child

Oh, how we planned and waited
For the moment of your birth.
Of all out little miracles,
You were the very first.
The first to hold, to raise, to love,
And fill our days with fun.
From your first tooth to your first steps,
We counted memories by so quickly.
And soon we realized,
Dear first born, you were growing up
Right before our eyes.
We have cherished every moment,
And we wanted you to know,
You have brought real joy into our lives,
And we love you so.

Our Middle Child

You were the second to be born.
How proud we were of you.
You were the answer to our prayers.
A special dream comes true,
And from the moment forward,
You have made life so much fun.
You have filled out hearts and lives with happiness,
And kept us on the run.
And for these special memories,
We have thanked the Lord above
For giving us a middle child.
To hold, to raise, to love.
We have cherished every moment,
And we wanted you to know
You have brought real joy into our lives,
And we love you so.

Perfect Love

That wedding day was remained pure.
Our loving hands were joined with eternal bonds,
Joined as one, hoping for a perfect life,
    with full assurance,
With tender charity, and faith.
Along with patient hope, and quiet, brave
    endurance,
With childlike trust, fearing no pain
    or death,
And granted joy which brightens sorrow,
And peace that calms strife.
It's still pure for you and me,
As our love for each other knows no ending.
That gives us eternal love and life.

Trust the Promises

My love for you is forever full,
Forever whole.
Nothing can turn me away.
Even through the nights of darkness,
Even if my friends forsake me.
But the sorrows will pass,
And I will go with you, and love you.
Trust the promises.
My love for you is forever full.
With my hands, I'll hold you.
In my arms, I'll fold you,
And I will not leave you.
I will not forget you,
But I will care for you.

Forever in Your Eyes

The sun, moon, and stars appear
    like a dream to me.
I'd give you my heart and soul
    if you'll show me the light to yours.
I'd keep you near to my heart
    if you'll love me forever.
For always, like the twinkle in your eyes
That will always shine bright.
I know true love will always be in my mind,
Because I know you'd be my first true love.
I'd do anything to try and make you happy.
I've never felt this way towards anyone,
For I lived in a world of my own,
And when I look into your eyes, I know exactly what I see…
I see forever in your eyes,
    for you and me.

Unbroken

Someone that you haven't even met wondered
        what it would be like to know someone like you.
Then two broken hearts found each other.
They healed each other.
Protected each other.
And loved each other.
You wanted me.
You wanted us.
You wanted it all.
With me, only me.

You accepted my past,
Supported my present,
And encouraged my future.
I only put work for you because you were the woman I wanted.
At the end of the day, I didn't remember beautiful faces.
I remembered you, with the most beautiful heart and soul.

We have been through the worst, and got the best.
We didn't have to always agree, but we learned to respect one another.
And our true love stood by each other's side

on good days and even closer on bad days.

Our true love was about growing as a couple.

Learning about each other.

And never giving up on each other.

We had a great relationship,

One that I never expected to be in.

It challenged my every view I had.

Your love was unconditional, and you carried heavy burdens.

My love for you was so real.

It revealed my heart would never stop beating for you.

Trust, respect, loyalty and communication was all that you asked of me.

But I made you feel unwanted and alone,

Especially when you were there.

Now that you're gone,

I never knew how great of a woman you are

Until I took it all for granted.

Now I realize, goodbyes aren't forever.

Isn't the end.

It simply means I'll miss you, until we meet again.

But remember, you'll always be the answer when somebody

asks me what I'm thinking about.

Your Marvelous Love

As I sat at the kitchen table,
Reflecting on all my years,
I questioned the times me and my family
Have suffered and wept bitter tears.

And wondering how much really mattered,
And how much meant nothing.
But was it worth all the heartaches and pain?
As many Sunday questions came.

I've also seen that there was a time in my life
When I was blinded.
The marvelous love of yours I could not see.
Then one day my eyes were opened.

And you even showed promise.
That's when your marvelous love shined on me.
Down in my heart.
From Heaven above.

But now I'm feeling sad and lonely.
A true and trusted friend I cannot find.
As I see that there's no greater love
Than your marvelous love.

But now I'm missing your marvelous love
As it keeps shining,
And once made me happy.
Oh, there's no greater love

As I see that my name may not be
Famous here.
But I do see that there's just no love
That's made me happier
Like your love.

My Own Foolish Pride

Over the years

She had tears to fall from her eyes.

But here she is, still by my side,

Never breaking the ties between her and I.

Though I've been selfish over those years, I've seen her radiant.

Still she loves me more than life itself.

And if you could just see the glow on her face,

Then you would understand

Why I've always concluded that she'd understand.

Even though she would, it still hurt her.

Oh, what I'd do for my own foolish pride.

Though at times I reached forward, to what lied ahead,

It's been hard for me to forget what lies behind me.

Now I try to be a good father and a good lover to their mother.

For I want to have to play catch up with my family,

Or make up for the lost time, because of my foolish pride.

As before, only tears fell from her eyes,

And my conclusion was that she understood.

Even though she would, and it hurt her still, I see now as I become this man they long for,

That when they speak, I'll listen.

Then I'll understand, and won't take them for granted

As I become a better father and lover for their mother.

A Few Years Ago

A few years ago,

I'd ask myself many of questions....

    Questions that seemed to have no answers.

Until you came into my life.

Never did I know that you were the answers.

In the darkest times,

It seemed that I couldn't find my way.

I was needing someone to say that they loved me.

A few years ago,

I felt hopeless in a hopeless world.

Then you took my hand in yours,

And the answers to my questions seemed clear.

For all of the questions that I had, you were the answer.

A few years ago,

I fell in love with you.

For my questions, which seemed to have no answers,

Were answered a few years ago,

When I fell in love with you.

PART TWO
WONDERS

Lonely Sidewalk

Walking along the lonely sidewalk,
Up in a distance, I saw a young boy.
The clothes he wore were torn and swayed in the breeze.
As we approached each other,
I noticed his feet were bare
And his face was pale and sad.
As we now stood face to face,
I felt bad seeing the child, the way he was.
So I told him my name.
And he never introduced himself to me.
We sat along the lonely sidewalk.
Then he began to talk.
He told me of his mother leaving a few months
      after his birth.
And in his eyes, I saw the tears which he
      held back.
Then after a while he began talking again.
He spoke of all the pain he's gone through,
And all the homes he's been in.
So it began to sink in. Now I understood,
The small boy was helpless at the age he was

Along that lonely sidewalk.

We talked.

And I listened, for I could relate.

It touched my heart, seeing this boy as he was.

I was a stranger to him, but he had talked anyway.

Rough boy, that's what he referred himself as.

Then I asked myself, why do things happen
      as this?

Helpless he seemed, but believe he did.

Someday, he said, maybe the world will see.

See the children crying for help.

As the boy looked at me one last time,

For me to see, that small boy was me.

That Man (That Came Between Us)

Today seems just like another day.
Another day for me to face alone.
Wondering why I wear this frown on my face.
From thinking about that man that came
    between you and me.
Yes, that man that put himself first.
That man that thought of only himself.
That man that made you lose your smile.
And now he's lost you, too.
That man's hand you held, that might have
    held you down.
Now I'm looking back on my life,
And all the things I don't agree with.
Thinking that I could've been a better friend
    to you.
Now I see without you,
This isn't the road I thought.
These aren't the dreams I bought.
And on this road I've taken, I've awakened.
Awakened to see I'm the man
    who came between us.

How Wonderful

As I look in the mirror,
Who do I see staring back at me?
A soul that's lost,
But controlled by a love in the making.
There's time for everything,
And work isn't always required,
Because there's such a thing as sacred idleness.
So, I awakened my confidence,
And those that I love will certainly flower,
But there's one that I love more than my skin.
And constant use hasn't worn ragged the fabric
      of our relationship.
But without her, I wonder how I could feel so small
      and so whole at the same time.
But these few lines are intended as a brief greeting.
I hope that she'll remember something for our meeting.
Maybe she'll keep in her mind a lasting echo,
      some human link.
For everybody breathes his soul into their work,
      his laughter, his joy, and his grief.
And how wonderful.

Special Children

This may sound
      a little sentimental,
but you're everything a parent
ever hopes their children will be.
You're understanding,
      kind, and honest,
and you give your best
      to everything you do.
It's no wonder warm
      and loving thoughts
come easily to mind
      when they're thoughts about
      special children as all of you.

Our Special Gift

The angels smiled when you were born,
      because they surely knew
It would be a very special day,
The day God sent us you.
We held you and we loved you,
      and from the very start,
We considered you a special gift.
      loved with all our hearts,
We have cherished every moment.
And we wanted you to know
You have brought real joy into our lives,
      and we love you so.

Don't You Worry, God Will See You Through

"Heartache and pain."
If you got a problem today and can't seem
    to find your way,
Or if you're depressed or your life seems worthless,
Don't you worry, God will see you through
    the heartaches and pain.
"Mama."
I look back on my life and all the things I've been through,
Deaths and depression, I must have been out of my mind.
Walking alone at times, it seemed.
Without a place to go, or a friend to turn to.
Any time of day, in the bitter cold,
        Don't you worry, God will see you through.

Master's

We are all prisoners,
Locked into a world of space
    and time.
We have control of our actions.
But our actions are actually our
    reactions.
To occurrences in time and space.
The pattern of which are sent by
    forces.
Beyond our very limited
    comprehension.
Each person in this world
Is here to find his way back
    to God.
God manifests into our lives.
Problems that we must solve and
    overcome.
In order to become masters of our
    own lives.
Once we have overcome the trials
    and tests

Given to us on earth.

We will then be able to become

    the company to God

That we originally were intended to be.

Wings That Will Set You Free

Another morning finds me
Another day to face alone.
Is there a memory where I use to be?
Or do you see me beyond the pain?
As these eyes reflect back at me.
I see half a man.
Some of my friends tell me that I need
      to forget you.
But they don't know what stands in my way.
And I'm wondering why I couldn't see
      what you meant to me.
It's better to have disappointments in love
      than never to have loved at all.
Don't judge our relationship because of one failure.
The best part of our lives we pass in,
      counting on what is to come.
Is it time that you need, or is it goodbye?
Do we let the love we made
      turn to memories?
Time for your broken wings to mend, and learn
      to fly again.
Wings that will set you free.

I Asked

I asked for strength.
You gave me difficulties to make me strong.
I asked for wisdom.
You gave me problems to solve.
I asked for prosperity.
You gave me brain, and brawn to work.
I asked for courage.
You gave me danger to overcome.
I asked for love.
You gave me trouble.
I asked for favors.
You gave me opportunities.
I received nothing I asked for
      and received everything I needed.

Destination Unknown

Destination unknown.
The words you spoke softly,
    softly, not wanting me to hear.
Time and time again.
The note that you wrote and left behind
    was all that you left for me.
My head hung down after I read the finely printed words.
You told me that I needed someone,
    someone who would love and understand me.
And if someday we should pass, for us not to look away
    as if we were strangers.
I raised my head up to see you
    in a picture.
Which then only memories came into
    my mind.
You told me not to search for you,
For your destination was unknown.
If only I could see you, I'd tell you that it's you
    who loves and understands me.
But you're gone.

Said it's something you had to do.
I ask myself how long do my tears have to fall?
A week? A month? Or even years?
You said that I needed someone who would love
    and understand me.
Someone who wouldn't hurt me anymore.
Maybe that someone was you, but how do I let you know?
When you have an unknown destination?
If only you would've given me forever,
    forever to share my love with you.
After a while my tear-streaked face began to smile
    from our memories.
Memories cherished in my heart,
But not strong enough to bring you back,
    back to the one who loves and understands you.
The one who asked for forever from you to share
    my love with.
Destination unknown.
Let it be me she'll find.

There's A Man (That I Call Dad)

There's a man who has lived his life dreaming.
He's fulfilled most every one of them.
He'd work from sunrise, to sunset,
Just to provide for his family.
His wife and him had been married thirty something years.
And his only son would soon be out of school and grown.
Then he, too, would have his dreams to fulfill for himself.
But that man had taught his son right from wrong.
That same man had run his fingers through fifty-five years of living.
And he told his son that he wouldn't always be by his side.
A few months later, their only son was graduating from high school.
His mother and dad smiled.
Knowing that he'd fulfilled one of his and their dreams.

Three months later, that man and his son
      shared the evening together.
They sat and talked.
And the boy's dad said son,
Be someone that somebody else will love
      and understand.

For me, that will fulfill my dreams.

Now that you're grown, and I'm about gone,

Do that for me, my only son.

It's hard not to tell you not to cry.

You're going to miss me, but let me go.

For my son, it's only Jesus coming.

I Keep Believing

Mama would ask me, is that another letter that
    you're writing to her?
I'd hesitate to answer,
If I answered at all.
Mama knows that I still love her, as I face every day
    alone.
Son, I know that you love her,
For it shows when you search for the words
    to write.
But there will be a day that you'll find another.
And you'd be a fool to take her back after all she's
    put you through.
Mama's words were so true, but words I don't want
    to hear.
And mama knows that I keep believing that one day
    she'll love me.
And I keep believing that every day.

No matter what I hear about her,
She's my first true love.
And not knowing where life would've taken us,
I keep believing that one day she'll be back.

I keep believing that our love is still eternal.

I know, my only son, that you still love her.

But if she loved you, she'd be here now.

Mama's words so true, but hard for me to swallow.

My only son, life is short.

Don't waste it abusing your heart, and don't get hurt
> no more by her.

Someday you'll find someone,

Someone who will love and understand you.

But I keep believing.

Day after day.

Time after time.

I keep on believing that she'll love me one day.

And that one day, she'll be back.

Mama knows the pain that my face has shown.

After our last good-byes,

I turned my head from mama, as I keep believing that
> we'll get it right one day.

But now my believing seems to be letting me
> down.

As I swallowed the words mama had spoken,
> words I didn't want to hear.

Remember Me

There's a man who has lived his life as a sinner and a thief.

And the world had seemed to push him away, to only judge him by his ways.

Then one day he learned of a man named Jesus, who was to be crucified.

The sinner traveled to Calvary to see this man named Jesus.

Once the sinner arrived at Calvary,

He saw Jesus crucified on the cross.

Then he walked towards Jesus, and fell to his knees.

And began to pray.

"Dear Jesus, please forgive me of my sins, and please remember me when you're in the heavens

    with thy father."

Jesus heard the sinner's prayer, and said to him,

"I've forgiven you; no longer will you be pushed away, and judged by your ways."

"But as I remember you."

"Remember me, and all the things that I've stood and stand for."

Remember me.

I Learned

I learned how to laugh.

I learned how to cry.

And I learned how to love.

I even learned how to lie.

Now my heart has been broken into,

And my nights are sleepless.

But I still reach out for you,

When I should be trying to forget you.

I try to find a loving letter, that my heart never sent,

And I think of all the things that you taught me,

Now that you're gone.

Because you'd think I could learn to tell you.

      goodbye.

When I Cry

Sometimes I cried.

It wasn't my bottle that I wanted.

Sometimes when I cried,

It wasn't that my diaper needed changing.

Sometimes when I cried,

It wasn't because I was hurting.

Now that I grew up a little more,

You may find me crying,

But it's not because I'm hungry.

Nor is it because my pull-up needs changing.

Nor am I hurting.

Sometimes when I cry,

I just need you to hold me,

And for you to give me some of your time,

And love.

Weeping Willow

With your tears running down,
Why so you always weep and frown?
Is it because he left you one day?
Is it because he could not stay?
On your branches he would swing.
Do you long for the happiness that day would bring?
He found shelter in your shade.
You thought his laughter would never fade.
Weeping willow stop your tears.
For there is something to calm your fears.
You think death has ripped you forever apart,
But I know he'll always be in your heart.

Treasure in Life

Many are the hardships in a vast, bitter land of suffering and strife,
    close companions to man challenging fate to control my own destiny.

I boldly offered her golden prosperity.

My elusive search began conquering many miles
    of earth.

I discovered a treasure, a woman of rare worth with eyes of richest sapphire,
    complexion of gold.

Yet, commitment had no place in my carefree world.

Adventure my first love, danger controlling my day.

Like money, love charms a dreamer, taking his freedom away.

Love accepted this challenge, my strong will to tame,

Though I must figure her changes, for I'm to
    blame.

A woman was molded from hardship and despair,

Even knowing me well, offered her heart with a dare.

Defeat glazes her eyes, her tears and dreams
    all spent.

Without ever knowing, she became my golden torment,

Now the moment has come when I must choose,

Which of these treasures I will recklessly lose?

My heart's not as frozen as a glacial frontier.

All I'm asking is

Will freedom be as golden when you're no longer here?

Daddy

First love.

First son.

Or perhaps a precious daughter.

There, laughter swift and sweet.

His hand so sure.

His love so pure.

His loyalty to them amazing.

His patience vast and his heart wider than the heavens
        above.

For their lives.

The bright sun in their eyes, the one to whom
        they turn.

The man for whom they burn, the flame of love
        so bright.

His wisdom always right.

His hand so strong, so seldom wrong.

So sweet, so near, so dear, so much the love of all.

And once upon a time so tall,

His love for them never ending, always entertaining.

Handsome, teaching, reaching for the stars, driving

funny cars.

A loving hand and heart for every loss of daddy.

Beloved man, eternal friend.

How lucky I am, sweet children, to be your daddy.

This Is Me

Here I am. This is the new me.

All for her, like she wants me to be.

Why do I change for her?

Just like she wants me.

Aged, tall, and thin.

The more I think about it,

        maybe this is me.

Growing up, maturing.

How I was meant to be.

Yes, that's what it is.

I'm so sure now.

This is me growing up.

Don't ask me how.

My personality changed so much from before.

I can't help but to choose to show

        disloyal friends to the door.

I realize after years of fake, shallow friends, and pain.

What true friends are.

They forever will remain

By my side, though I kicked others out,

        so old friends shouldn't blame her.

I can't help what I'm about.

Letters from War

As he rode away,
She fell to her knees,
And began to pray to the Heavenly Father above,
For she asked Him to give her son His almighty
    bravery, strength, and love.
Feeling so alone and afraid,
But more scared for her son.
She went out to her mailbox,
And found a letter from war.
This is what it said:
Mam, I'm doing all right.
Don't be afraid or scared,
For I'm defending our country and freedom.
And he closed it with "I love you."
As she folded the letter from war,
She paused to wipe the misty tears from her eyes,
Then looked up to the Heaven above.
A few months had passed by.
As before, she received yet another letter from war.
She opened it carefully and started reading.

Mam, our platoon was attacked today,
And your son didn't run away,
But instead he stayed, and helped the wounded.
He was brave, so the letter from war ended.
With that, she began to cry,
As she held the letter from war,
Then she looked above, and asked of the Father
    His love.
As a few weeks passed by,
She looked out of her door to see a corporal,
Where her son once stood.
So she went out to greet him,
And here's what he said:
Ma'am, I know that you received the letters from
    war,
And as you've commanded,
I've returned home safely to you,
As before, all I could do was write a letter
    from war.

Making of a Dad

God took the strength of a mountain,

The majesty of a tree,

The warmth of a summer sun,

The calm of a quite sea,

The generous soul of nature,

The comforting arm of night,

The wisdom of ages,

The power of the eagle's flight,

The joy of a morning in spring,

The patience of eternity,

The depth of a family need.

God combined these qualities.

When there was nothing more to add,

He knew His masterpiece was complete,

And so He called it………. Dad.

The Strength to Meet Life's Challenges

Your stronger than you think.
Remember to stand tall.
Every challenge in your life
    helps you to grow.
Every problem you encounter
    strengthens your mind and soul.
Every trouble you overcome
    increases your understanding of life.
When all your troubles weigh heavily
    on your shoulders,
Remember that beneath the burden,
    you can stand tall,
Because your never given
    more than you can handle,
And you're stronger than you think.
I believe in you and all you can do!

Come and Be with Me

I'm sitting here wondering how it would be.

How it would be just to touch you.

I'd tell you of my dreams

And of my love that you could rely on.

In my eyes you would see our future.

How far it seems, amidst the time until then.

Until then, we'll make mistakes,

Mistakes unattended to break on another's heart.

But understand as you take my hand,

Unity is a rare gift among few.

Come and be with me.

As we sit side by side, as if you'll stand by my side.

Stand by my side, as I'll know that my eternal dream is being with you.

You'll see, for me it's hope.

For my belief is stronger than my advice.

Now that I've found where I belong, will you come and be with me?

For if you feel the same, I'll see our future in your eyes.

But far as it may seem, amidst the time until then,

Come and be with me.

And in our eyes, we'll see our future.

Far as it may seem, amidst the time until then come and be with me
And in our eyes, we'll see our future.
Though far as it may seem, amidst the time until then,
For many distant miles it may seem,
Come and let us be.

Open My Eyes

Open my eyes so that I may see
And be set free.
Open my ears so that I may hear
And everything false will disappear.
Open my mouth and let me speak truth.
Open my heart so that I can prepare a love
To share with my children.

In My Dreams

There's a woman
Who says she loves me.
She's standing on a falling star,
And I'm not sure what that means.
She has kissed me
On a mountain,
Several miles above the sea.
She has laid me on a bed of leaves
And loved me in a tree.
In my heart, I feel her laughing,
And in my ears, I hear her sing.
While her echoes fill the canyon walls,
I weave a wedding ring.
Far away, she kneels above me
As I fall back to the light.
With my will I try to hold onto
My beautiful lover of the night.

Empty Heart

I see the path that I've sought is hidden from me

Now that I've let you down.

Even though you trusted and believed in me.

There were things that I hid from you,

But I can't hide the shame.

And I wished that someone could take away the pain,

Because without a light, I fear that I will stumble

     in the dark,

And I'll stay down and decide not to go on

Because I feel that I lost myself.

And my courage is soon to follow.

Oh, I'm a soldier

Wounded so I must give up the fight.

There's nothing more for me.

So lead me away, or just leave me lying here.

For there is not a road that I know

That leads to anywhere.

And that's when somewhere on high

     in a distance,

A voice says, "Remember who you are."

But as seasons change,
I remember how I use to be,
Because I can't go on, I can't even start,
Because I've got nothing left, just an empty heart.

My Last Day

When I lost my way,

You were my light.

And when the world done me wrong,

You done me right.

When I look into your eyes,

You don't tell me lies.

You tell me the truth.

You always get me through.

Now this is what I got,

And this is what say.

If this were my last day,

Going down this road,

All I got is my world.

And I'll give it all to you.

Because you've never broke my heart.

If this was my last day,

My last breath,

Or my last chance,

This is what I'd say.

Thank you for the laughter.

And I'm sorry for the tears.

And I'd say goodbye to all those years,
Because I know that it was your heart
    that got broke.

A Heart of a Woman

The days and nights,
I sit around wondering.
Where can she be?
I hope that she'll appear out of nowhere.
But I fail to see
All the hurt inside and wounded pride.

Oh, what she went through for me.
I cheated, and lied,
And our love slowly died.
As her heart broke in two,
When she was with me.
All above, behind me.

Right or wrong,
She tried to hold on.
Hold on.
I went too far, now she's gone.
It's over, and her hearts turned to share,
With no pity.

When her heart turned to stone.
She cried a little,
As her heart her turned to stone.
She's that kind of woman.
She'll do fine on her own.
I thought that it was a game.
A game that I was winning.
But I wouldn't go my way.
So I lost what I had.
Now I'm back at the beginning.
And that's the price I've got to pay.

When she was with me,
All alone, behind me,
Right or wrong,
She tried to hold on.
Hold on.
But I went too far, and now she's gone.

Now it's over.
As her heart turned to stone,
No time for pity.
She'll cry sometimes.

But she's a woman now.
And the sad thing to see is
A heart turn to stone.
But that's a heart of a woman.

8 x 10

He sees an 8 x 10 of two great kids and himself,
And his wife.
Then he wonders why
She's not there.
As his tears fell on lovesick letters,
He searched his heart, but had no clue.
But he couldn't surrender, because he remembered
How her love branded his heart.
Then he thought about how she might get on
With her life.
But she knows that temptations are out there waiting.
And he won't see when she starts falling.
But if he could see her,
He'd tell her,
It's a long way down, and a hand road back.
And no fates too uncertain, no distance too far.
As you find a war to give back what it takes.
But his tears only fell on lovesick letters
As he looked at an 8x10 of two great kids,
And himself and his wife.

Twenty-Three

I've seen pictures of you.
> pictures which were unable to show me a thousand words.

And in my mind, I try to see how your face
Would have aged in the twenty-three years of my life.
But as I grew older, I was told stories about you.
Of you leaving me, going to another place.
But still I try to place your face in my life
> after twenty-three years.

Were things so bad to leave your baby son?
So alone in this world underneath my fears.
And still I wonder as the days pass me by,
> did you ever shed a tear for me?

I've only dreamed of seeing your face one day.
But I know that one day, we'll meet
> face to face.

And don't think that these twenty-three years
> can be restored in a day.

Only if that day comes that we should meet,
> don't let it take you by surprise.

If your baby boy says nothing at all, but why?

One Shining Moment

Time is short,
And the road is long.
In the blink of an eye,
The moment you thought would be, are gone.
And when it's done,
You hurt deep down inside.
You feel that you did your best
And all those years.
No one really knows just how hard you've tried.
But I see it show.
Your heart is not open.
But there I still stand, believing.
You feel that you have to run,
But where will you run to, when there's no place
      left to hide?
I've longed to feel your heart beating
And to see the beauty of your face, day after day.
It's more than just holding you,
And more than worrying about someone taking your place.
One shining moment, you reached for the sky,
But were you willing to try to love me
As I love you.

Father-Children

I used to wipe milk from their mouths,
Now they're wiping milk from mine.
That was when we were both younger.
Seems like a short, short time.
I used to wrap them with a blanket
At night as they watched t.v.
But now my bones are old and cold,
And they tuck a blanket around me.
I used to hold their hands so tight.
When we had to cross each street,
Now they softly grasp my hand
At every corner that we meet.
I used to check on them at night
And kiss their checks so tenderly.
Now they help me into bed,
And how tenderly they kiss me.
I used to teach them things I knew,
Like how to jump, skip, and throw.
But now they have to remind me at times,
"Dad, this is someone you know."
I used to be their everything,

A hero, chauffeur.
But now it seems I would be nothing
If it weren't for them.
Time has a way of reversing roles
To where we're not what we seem to be.
I was the father; now I'm the child.
The ones I cared for now care for me.
I used to be someone long ago.
That, well, I can't seem to recall.
But as I look into their loving faces,
Whatever I was, was worth it all.

Look to This Day

Look to this day,

For it is life.

The very life of life.

In its brief course lie all.

The realities and verities of existence.

The bliss of growth.

The splendor of action.

The glory of power.

For yesterday is but a dream,

And tomorrow is only a vision.

But today, well lived,

Makes every yesterday a dream of happiness.

And every tomorrow a vision of hope.

Look well, therefore, to this day.

Girl on The Moon

It was a Sunday, a day just like any other

When you left.

Oh, it doesn't feel right.

As I daydream,

I think of the hard times, which we refused to draw a line to.

Now my mind is wandering

As I look for a face

That I can't never find.

And her hand reaches for me,

But like the desert sand, it sifts away.

Oh, my girl on the moon,

I'll put a candle in the window,

So that you'll find your way back to me.

But maybe you're thinking of another.

But I'm looking for a love that'll last.

Oh, my girl on the moon,

Am I looking too hard?

Or in a matter of time,

Will I find you to love again?

Because you're warm and true.

But am I wrong,

My girl on the moon?

In His Care

Where am I going?
Which path will I take?
These questions I ask myself
As I know that my destination isn't a place,
    but within the activity of today.
So if you sit and wonder of tomorrow, my child,
You'll miss your destination in today.
So if you must wonder, wonder not at
    where you are going.
But how far you have traveled to arrive in today.

Under the Milky Way

Do you remember once upon a time?
When you were mine?
The stars above were bright and new,
I pulled them down for you.
Just when I fell in love again.
Now I only wished that I knew
What you were looking for.
Might I know what you will find?
Because it feels so empty,
As the sounds of our breathes fade with the lights.
And to you it seems there's nothing.
But a slow blowing dream
That your fear tries to hide
Deep inside of your mind.
As you cry all along, those silent tears,
I only wished that I knew what you were looking for.
Might I know what you will find?
Despite your destination,
And the sounds of our breaths fading with the lights.
Is it something shimmering and white

That led you here?

Because the stars are bright and new.

So do you long for me to pull them down for you?

Here under the Milky Way tonight?

Keep This Address

Today, Dear Lord, I'm 30 and there's much
    I haven't done.
I hope, Dear Lord, you'll let me live until
    I'm 31.
But then, if I haven't finished all I want to do,
Would you let me stay until I'm 32?
So many places I want to go, so very
    much to see.
Do you think, Dear Lord, you could leave
    me here though 33?
The world is changing very fast, with
    so much more in store,
I guess I'd like it very much to live
    until I'm 34.
And if by then I'm still alive, I'd
    like to stay till 35.
I know it must be really nice to be
    up there in Heaven,
But how about getting me through 36 and 37?
By then I'll be slowing down and often late.
Even so, I can't imagine not being here at 38.

Then again, it would be fine to celebrate number 39.

I guess, Dear Lord, I'll thank you kindly,

If you let me keep this address 'til

I'm well past 40.

Be

Be true, for there are those who trust you.

Be pure, for there are those who care.

Be strong, for there is much to suffer.

Be brave, for there is much to dare.

Be a friend, for all --- even the foe, the friendless.

Be giving, forget the gift.

Be humble, for you know your weakness.

Look up and laugh and love and lift.

Be tuned in to hear the slightest whisper.

Be faithful, to keep the path straight.

Standing on Promises

I've been standing on the promises,
On promises that can't fail.
Even when the howling storms of doubt and
      fear assails.
I shall prevail.
Standing on promises,
Bound to love's strong card,
Daily overcoming, for I can't fail.
Listening every moment to the calling,
As I stand on promises.

Your Best

Do your best.
Be it great or small.
It's a test, but be the best you can.
Not for rewards, or praise of man.
Your talents may be few,
They may be small,
Be good and true.
In all that you do or think,
Do your best, your all.

Be Brave, Be True

Strive to be right.

Fight bravely and be strong.

Fear only what's wrong.

Dare to be brave.

Dare to be true.

They'll be trials to overcome.

But never let your grace or your own self fail.

God grant you the courage to carry you through.

For He knows your heart,

And He never fails.

Remember to help others.

Forever be kind.

Let others see a strong friend in you.

Fight and be brave.

Your mighty heart will save.

Not Yet

I was a ball of clay, when He took
      me up in His hands.
He squeezed and patted me.
I asked him to stop.
But He only smiled at me and said Not Yet.
After a while He put into a kiln.
It was hot.
He took me out and set me on a wooden table.
Then began painting me.
I asked Him to stop, as the paint fumes made me dizzy and faint.
But He said Not Yet.
When He was through, He placed me back into the kiln.
I asked Him to let me out, but He only smiled and said Not Yet.
After a while He took me out and sat me on a shelf.
He picked up a mirror so that I could see myself.
And He explained that when He squeezed and patted me,
That He was making me.
And when He put me into the kiln it made me strong,
And when He painted me though it made me dizzy and faint,
He put color into my life.
And through it all I was in His hands the whole time.

I Never Thought

There was something there between us,
But you can't see it now with your eyes.
But in my heart, I see it all.
Though we've said goodbye,
It still reminds me of the time of my life.
As we turned our own ways, and walked away.
Unknowing how our lives without each other would be.
I never thought I'd get over you, but now only
        memories remain.
I never thought that one day we'd say goodbye.
But what a blow I took, when you said goodbye.
Goodbye, I never said. For me, it was forever.
I never thought I'd be able to laugh again.
After we said our last goodbyes.
And all that I never thought I could do without you,
        I'm doing.
Life for me isn't the same, but I know it's changed.
With the word "goodbye."
When you look into my eyes, you'll see the light still shines,
For I can't let your last goodbye get me down.
Because if I do, I'll get behind.

Give Your Best

Give your best of your youth.
Throw your soul in the battle for truth.
Be an example, young and brave.
Give loyalty devotion.
Give the best you have.
And know it within your heart.
Give and to you shall be given.
Gratefully seek while you give your best.
Nothing else is worthy, but your love.
Give glory to the Man above.
Give from your heart.
But do so with your best.
Give with the strength of your youth.
And join in the battle of truth.

Weary

Bring your wounded hearts,

For there's no sorrows that Heaven cannot heal.

Come to the feast of love.

Give the straying light.

Earth has no sorrows that Heaven cannot cure.

Earth has no sorrows, that Heaven can't remove.

Above speaks the comforter.

New Beginning

It's a new beginning, though maybe unseen.

Through all of my sin,

But I've been pardoned,

I've been moved by His divine compassion.

He died for my heart to win.

And I've been crowned.

The angels are crying.

Angels are around us, also.

And when He appears, His image I shall bear

In my soul and body.

To Christ, love and praise belong.

Another Year

Another year is dawning, let it be.

In working or waiting,

Another year with you,

Another year of progress and proving

Which is presence all the days.

Another year of faithfulness and gladness.

Another year of leaning upon your loving breast.

Another year of trusting and service.

Another year is dawning on earth, in Heaven,

Another year for you.

As We Await Your Return

Caught in the traffic of daily distresses,
Trapped in routines that have lost their appeal,
Weary of holding to dreams that elude us,
As we await you return.
Jaded by broken commitments and loses,
Reeling from setbacks that rob our reserves,
Fearing the words of a doctor's announcement,
as we await your return.
Troubled by cultural trends that are godless,
Doubting decisions, the courts claim as fair,
Haunted by laughter that mocks moral wisdom,
We await your return.
Longing for what God intended in Eden,
Hopeful for meaning beyond what we see,
Looking for ultimate justice and mercy,
As we await your return
LORD JESUS.

PART THREE
SORROW

I Think About Us

I think about a stranger

That I met years ago.

Yes, I'm thinking about us.

I think of the love that we've got

    for our children.

I think about how I'm wrapped around

    your finger.

And I also think about how you left,

    without saying a word.

But I can't stop loving you.

As I think about us.

I Was Wrong

As she's passing away,
I stood here lonely, with fear,
Looking for the light.
But people tell me that she can't hear me now.
Remembering how she'd smile for me
As I held her hand.
But I guess now her last lonely teardrop fell.
And I knew I've never been so loved.
Living without her touch
And her loving arms which surrounded me,
That wouldn't let me fall.
I see that I was wrong.
Yeah, I see that I was wrong.
And if I could only go back in time,
Back when she was mine,
When she held my hand,
And I was her man,
And just to be with her.
Maybe she had her doubts,
But if she'd put her trust in me,

When I say, I see that I was wrong,

Maybe only then she'd feel that she could stay forever.

But only now it's her memory that's coming back to me.

I Should've Been There

As a small child,
I walked down what seemed to be, a long aisle.
At the end, I looked up and watched the cross,
And as I began to shed my tears,
I thought, I should've been there on the cross,
With the crown of thorns on my head,
But I only shuddered.
I thought about how they gambled for his clothes,
As my heart got heavy.
I then imagined them piercing his side,
As I cried.
After that there was no more to see.
As I turned away wondering what life was worth
      living for.
Then after a few days had passed,
I knew what life was worth living for.
He had risen.

The Borrowed Child

I'll lend for you a little child of mine, He said.

For you to love the while he lives and mourn for when he's dead.

It may be six or seven years or twenty-two or three.

But will you, till I call him back, take care of him for me?

He'll bring his charms to gladden you, and should his stay be brief.

You'll have his lovely memories as solace for your grief.

I cannot promise he will stay, since all from earth return.

But there are lessons taught down there that I want this child to learn.

I've looked this wide world over in my search for teachers true.

And from the throngs that crowd life's lanes,

I have selected you.

Now will you give him all your love, nor think the labor vain.

Nor hate me when I come to take him back home again.

I fancied that I heard thee say,

Dear Lord, thy will be done,

For all the joy thy child shall bring, the risk of grief we'll run.

We'll shelter him with tenderness, we'll love him while we may.

And for the happiness we've known forever grateful stay.

But should the angels call for him much sooner than we've planned,

We'll brave the bitter grief that comes and try to understand.

When I Cry

I'm sorry that I'm late,

But I had to go by and see another friend.

Though I already said good-bye.

Nothing left to say.

Well before I begin to cry.

Here are some flowers

That I bought an hour ago.

It doesn't seem that far back

When you and I laughed

And had our talks together.

I also remember us taking those walks

On those cooler days.

Now that I'm older,

I find those words that I never said to you

Have melted into pure gold.

Well, I see the gate keeper motioning to me.

So I guess I must go now.

But once again, I'm sorry that I was late,

And I know that I already said good-bye.

But I always find something to say.

Even if it's nothing more than my tears,

    when I cry.

Depending on You

Went to the hospital,
Two weeks before daddy passed away.
Daddy said, son, I want to talk to you.
The first thing daddy told me, He said, son, I'm
      proud of you.
He said, you took me all over the country.
He said, if I needed some water, you were there.
If I needed food, you were there.
He said, as long as you live, I'll never die.
He said, you walk like me.
He said, you talk like me.
He said, you look like me.
He said, there's something I want you to do.
I said, what's that, daddy?
Daddy said, I'm depending on you to pull the family
      through.
I'm depending on you to pull the family through.
Then he said, take care of your mother, son,
Like I've always done.
He said, the reason I'm asking you this

He said, is that you are my only son.
He said, I married your mother I was only fifteen.
He said, all of your mother's life, she always depended on me.
So I'm depending on you to pull the family through.
I'm depending on you to pull the family through.
He said in his dying hours, I don't want
    y'all to cry.
He said, y'all don't have to wash the tears from
    my eyes.
He said, I don't want you in the hospital,
With your head hung down.
He said, every time y'all get on the float,
I want you to sing until the tower, the tower comes
    down.
He said, I'm depending on you to pull the family through,
I'm depending on you to pull the family through.
And when I left, I felt like a weight.
I want to know, has anybody ever had weight
    on their shoulder?
So I went home and I picked up my Bible,
And I read where it says, not let thyself be troubled,
And I also read where it says look to the hill
    whence come at my health.

See, all my health comes from the Lord.

I got down on my knees.

I didn't waste any time. I got all the way down
    on my knees.

And I said, Jesus, I'm counting on you.

I don't have nobody else.

And when I stood up, I threw my arms towards
    Heaven.

And I said, Jesus, I'm depending on you to pull
    the family through.

I'm depending on you to pull the family through.

I want to know who has somebody depending
    on them.

See, you can't make it by yourself.

You can't carry that load.

You ought to raise your hands.

Raise your hands.

And say, Lord, I'm depending on you

to pull the family through.

Daddy

Looking at Daddy's scrap book, aged of yellow,

I see a sweet old-fashioned fellow.

A photo as he fishes and whistles, enjoying the simple life.

Presenting mom with a ring, making her his wife.

Daddy smoking cigarettes, picking sunflowers, too.

Daddy wearing flannel shirts and overalls of blue.

Chopping wood and placing it in a neat stack.

Angels taketh him away

      and memory brings him back.

The Morning Light

The morning light is breaking, as the darkness
    disappears.
We are waking to potential tears.
Each breeze that sweeps the land across
    nations in commotion.
Dews of grace came over us, and many in
    gentle showers.
And brighter scenes are opening every hour.
Cries to Heaven in return for abundant answers.
See, the nation is bending and those we love.
A thousand hearts above, while sinners now
    confess.

When Morning Comes

When the morning comes and I awake in my house,
I'll tell the story of how I overcame,
of how my cherished plans have failed
By disappointments that prevailed.
And how I wandered into darkness,
Heavy hearted and alone,
Hoping to understand it better.
And how temptations and hidden snares
have taken me by unawareness.
Trials seem dark on every hand,
I can't understand,
Looking at the ways that lead to the promised land.
But I still follow until I die,
Hoping to understand it better.
My heart has bled from thoughtless words
      and deeds.
And I wonder why the test,
Even when I try my best.
But I'm sure I'll understand it better.

The Last Hour

With pleasures forbidden,

Would this vain world charm,

To spread and work me harm,

Or bring to me remembrance?

Even in my last hour with strife and pain.

And when my dust returns to dust again,

In the hour of trial,

Would Jesus plead for me?

Or when He recalls my life,

Deny and depart from me,

For fear and favor suffer me to fall?

Jesus take me, dying, to eternal life.

Empty-Handed

When I must go
At my death, don't you shrink, nor falter.
Thoughts no longer cloud my brow.
The years of sinning, wasted,
But I could've recalled them all.
I would have done things differently
And gladly bow.
For I am saved now.
Get up and work until your day
Until night of death takes you, too.
But remember, don't empty- handed go.

He'll Take Care of You

Don't be dismayed.
Abide through the days.
And when your heart seems to fail,
Or when dangers fierce your path,
All you may need He'll provide.
Nothing that you ask will be denied,
No matter what the test may be.
Lean weary one upon His breast,
Through every day,
All the way.
So, don't be dismayed.
He'll take care of you.

I'm Still Here

Don't mourn, I'm not gone,
For the best thing has happened to me.
God's called me home.
I'm still here, though I may not be in your sight.
Don't worry about me.
Just put your faith in the Lord,
And everything will be all right.
My soul will be with everyone
Through each and every night.
When my death is too much to bear,
Drop on your knees and pray.

I Do Not Go Alone

If death should beckon me with outstretched hands,
And whisper softly of "An Unknown Land,"
I shall not be afraid to go.
For though the path I do not know,
I take death's hand without fear.
For He who safely brought me
Will also take me safely back.
And though in many things I lack,
He will not let me go alone
Into the valley that's unknown.
So I reach out and take Death's hand
And journey to the Promised Land.
I will always love you all.

Death is Only a Part of Life

We enter this world

From the Great Unknown,

And God gives each spirit

A form of its own,

He endorses this form

With a heart and soul,

To spur man on to his ultimate goal.

For all men are destined

To return as they came.

And birth and death

Are in essence the same.

And man is but born

To die and arise.

For beyond this world

In beauty there lies.

The purpose of death

Which is but to gain

Life everlasting in God's great domain.

And no one makes

This journey alone,

For God promised to take care of His own.

My Silent Cry

You were a young man,

Easy to understand,

And your smile was the light, to a dark man's soul.

Your life had many more years

And your dreams seemed endless.

You were my friend, indeed.

And your brown eyes stole many hearts.

Our time together wasn't wasted, but cherished.

Then soon to be memories.

As I watched you grow in every aspect of life,

Not only was I proud of you,

But so were the others

Who loved you more than any words,

Or life itself.

Then that day came,

When there were no last goodbyes.

And my life seemed empty

Underneath my silent cry.

My friend went home in Heaven,

Where I know he's got more friends,

And saw God.

But in my heart, there will always be a place for you.

Though we never said goodbye.

I think you hear it when I silently cry, from missing you.

And my words which I never told you, melted into pure gold.

But if my tears could build a staircase,

I'd go to Heaven and bring you back.

But I know that angels taketh you away,

And the memories bring you back.

A Child of God

Whether you were wedded or divorced,

Did you consider your decision?

Or live out your choices.

Did you think long, and hard enough?

Or was time to short, and felt wasted.

Or did you say, "I've got enough time?"

Underneath was there fear within you tears?

Or did you see the years, which you and I would grow.

I was to be a child of God's, but now that's gone.

Unborn, I'm home with our Father.

Did you ever wonder who I'd be named?

Or was the shame,

The blame?

Was you afraid that I might cry, too often?

Or did you ever wonder how my soft skin may have felt?

I was special,

But you'll never know.

Have you ever wondered, what I might have been?

Now that you've committed the sin?

I would've been your best friend,

And I could've warmed your heart.

But we shall never know.

For all these things

I'm now doing in Heaven above.

Never Alone

I'm never alone in the morning,

As I rise at the break of dawn.

For Jesus who watched through the darkness

Says "Lo, I'm with you always."

I'm never alone at my table,

Though loved ones no longer I see.

For dearer than all who have vanished

Is Jesus who breaks bread with me.

I'm never alone through the daylight,

Though nothing but trials I see,

Though the furnace be seven times heated,

The form of the forth walks with me.

I'm never alone at the twilight.

When the darkness around me doth creep

And specters press hard round my pillow.,

He watches and cares while I sleep.

I'm walking and talking with Jesus

Each day as I travel along.

I'm never alone,

For the joy of the Lord is my song

Part Four

Lost Poems of Love

All don't deserve all places

  In my life.

If you want to be in any place,

  you have to earn it.

If you can't earn it.

Then respect it when I offer

  you that place.

It's said that a picture is worth a thousand words.

But when I saw yours,

  It was more than words could explain.

Your charming beauty within your pictures are irresistible.

I could wish you Prosperity, but I wish you Opportunities.

I could wish you Joy, but I wish you Courage.

I could wish you Happiness, but I wish you Wisdom.

……. to spot the opportunity and have the courage to follow through and may that be the source of your prosperity, happiness and joy.

Her soul is stained with yesterday's dust.

Her heart is stitched together with good intentions.

She has had her fair share of heartache.

Too many have misused her trust.

Still she shines from inside out.

Tearing the stars from her own soul on a clear night.

Hanging them in the sky to guide me home.

Feels like I knew you in a past life.

You and I seem so natural.

How I feel with you.

It feels good just being real.

All I ever wanted.

All I ever have been looking for.

Is the comfort of feeling safe,

 with you.

I reach out for your love.

A love so strong.

Which comes from your heart.

Not just from thoughts.

I'll be with you.

Not as a love seeker.

But as a love finder and keeper.

As I finally find home,

 in you.

At rising dawn.

You're like the warm sun.

In a pasture of sprouted flowers.

Where a million dreams.

Open like a scenery of fantasy.

You're full of love.

For me in my heart.

Where wishes are caressed.

Leaving love and memories.

With your hands.

Giving me moments that warms my heart.

As I love you passionately.

And sleep comes within the night.

When I saw you.

I felt a great need for you.

In your eyes you were hiding the pain.

I felt it without words.

I built up feelings.

Though some will want to own you.

Use you.

And abuse you.

Leaving your happiness.

Into sadness.

Because cheating love brings more suffering.

Knowing that pain is better,

 than picking up sadness.

All because love has been broken.

This is why love is just a dream.

Unfulfilled dreams.

You're lonely and distant from warm hands.

No matter how much we love each other.

You lived on memories.

If you ever chose to fly.

Fly with choices.

Not with wings that didn't try.

Our love isn't broken within all of this.

Because here we are.

Another long day waiting.

But this is how our life is going.

Patience is a virtue.

So I'll never be fed up,

  waiting.

For You.

You've brought me back to life.

Set my heart on fire.

You're my light.

I need you to warm these lonely nights.

Your body is like the holy grail.

I've got to find it.

As you love me like you do.

And find trust in whenI say,

 I love you.

Learn from my heart.

For me to forget where my end is.

For you to forget when you begin.

Make me feel your hands around me.

I can't imagine my life without you.

In this life your love is only what matters to me.

Love which fills my life, makes my heart beat.

When I am listening to your soft love whispers.

Your touch warms my heart.

There is nothing beautiful as surrendering to you.

Your love makes me alive.

You make my heart burn.

With love fire lasting to the end of time.

I can see in your eyes us, our love.

You are my flower, my love forever……

I know that times are changing.

For something new.

That means you too.

What started out as friendship.

Has grown stronger.

Even though you've been through hell.

Holding the ashes to prove it.

You have scars.

I subdued my fears.

Never wanting to cause you any sorrow.

Or pain.

Instead see you smiling.

Because you're not meant to be broken forever.

I'm not trying to fix you.

I can't heal you.

I'm just trying to show you.

How beautiful your broken is.

Each piece fits into a masterpiece,

 of who you are now.

Right now, I see a beautiful soul.

You love deep.

You've given people all of your light.

You want others to think you can't be hurt.

But, the truth is.

You hurt easier than most.

Even though you're fierce and tender.

Within the same breath.

This is your beauty.

Therefore sweet contentment and all things of soulful beauty.

Will always find you.

At night I dream of us.

Our bodies entangled in bed.

I can still taste your kiss.

Feel your breath on my skin.

The touch of my hands.

Sliding down your body.

As you whisper my name.

Longing to feel my strength in you.

I wish we were in the flesh.

Just let me dream.

Unless you're lying here beside me.

Reliving them instead.

Because these are not moments.

That i wish to miss.

When the sun shines,

  we shine together.

Told you I'll be here,

  Forever.

I'll always be your friend.

Took an oath that I'm sticking out.

Until the end.

You are my first experience with everything.

Love, intimacy and heartbreak.

No other woman has ever measured up to

 what you give me.

Or how you make me feel.

Make me wish.

Or let me dream.

Of a steamy passion.

Wanting to scream.

Just making me touch.

Your precious folds.

Where even in silence.

Our love unfolds.

Come let me taste your lips.

Let me find them sweet.

As our bodies get wrapped up in pleasure.

Entangled in the sheets.

One touch of your body.

Will leave me trembling with desire.

When you gaze into my eyes.

My heart beats faster.

With the thought of you.

Craving to be your slave.

Thriving to please my master.

Come let me taste your body.

Let me find out if its taste is sweet.

Which is sure to bring us to ecstasy.

Making us feel we're in heat.

All this time that you've been waiting.

You don't have to wait any longer.

Here in my arms is where you should be.

Because your love makes me believe.

No ocean or mountain can keep us apart.

I'm giving you my heart forever.

Every breath I take, I take for you and me.

That's a promise I'll keep.

Love like ours is hard to find.

I can't keep you off of my mind.

Every night I think of you.

Under stars twinkling high above.

I know that there's a million stars between us.

You make me complete.

This love I feel is so strong.

With you my heart found a home.

I know we'll be together forever.

Loving you faithfully.

You're my Angel.

You've given me wings.

And if there's one thing in this world that I know is true.

It's the love that I feel when I'm thinking of you.

Just as sand sifts through an hourglass.

Our time together drifts away from us,

  to become only memories.

When I see your beautiful face.

Everything on my mind is erased.

Then I go to that special place where it's only you and I.

Hand in hand.

In deep green forest.

On shores of sand.

I'd even write your name in the sky,

  but why?

When a cloud would remove it.

I'd write your name in the sand, but the wind would blow it away.

I'd write your name in my heart so nothing could remove it.

And when memories are all that's left.

In my heart you will be moving forward.

You with me or me with you.

And in Heaven too, you shall have my hand.

It's not mine to take.

Do I stand tall, or fall?

People say that I care.

But nothing do I give.

They say I have purpose.

Yet, just want me to live.

Oh, how I've lived for others.

Have I lived because I'm weak?

Or lived to only die inside?

I sit and I welcome……

Waiting for the day.

I give into defeat.

As within my mind.

I think I truly did belong.

As I decay.

My love for you has no beginning,

 or end.

But between remembering and forgetting.

It could be hurt or crushed.

Or blown away and suffer in silence.

But it lies within your heart with understanding.

With that kind of love for you.

I feel wonderful.

Even with tears I shed.

Time seems wasted.

The silence betrayed or distance forgotten.

Feel my love within your heart,

 with understanding.

That way regardless of how far you are.

You'll know it's true.

It's real.

If only you could see,

  through my eyes.

Then you'd know,

  that being with you.

Is an endless adventure.

The journey we're traveling on,

  to each town, city or state.

  wouldn't look the same,

  If you weren't by my side.

To experience all of the wonders,

  of this world.

There's no greater beauty,

  than sharing each moment with you.

Shimmering love.

You came along and broke my hopelessness.

You came and saved me.

Love has since blossomed within our friendship.

Take me where we can be alone.

Let me hold you in my arms.

As you softly whisper.

But it's just a dream, I think about.

Maybe I'm in love.

Because your memory is in my soul.

I'll never forget the day we started talking.

Because that day I met my best friend.

Somebody that I want to have in my life,
 forever.

And I'll forever be grateful for that day.

Because I met you.

For all this searching you're the best thing,
 that I've found.

I don't always find the words to say.

But I think about you constantly.

Rather it's with my mind,
 or my heart.

And it assures me that I'm never alone.

I'm a huge fan of who I'm becoming.

He's good.

He's happy.

He's trying to do great things.

I like him.

Don't worry about me.

Nor be concerned.

I knew it was a challenge.

Yet so much I learned.

I'm going to be alright.

We're not saying goodbye.

So I'm not going to cry.

But if I happen to.

I know I'll see your reflection,

 in each teardrop.

I'm going to be alright.

I just hope that you find your way.

Out of the darkness that surrounds you.

And find your way into the light.

Paint us on a midnight canvas.

With you catching me like a falling star.

Or us meeting under the stars twinkling.

Where nothing comes between us to unsettle.

And it becomes our secret sanctuary of love.

Where it's only us and the moon above.

With magic in the air between us.

And nobody hears the whispers of our hearts,

I know you've experienced a lot.

Tried turning your anger into peace.

You've made me proud.

You're the greatest.

Even though your name is in the streets.

With every new day, I try to maintain.

Just remember that your brother and I have been there.

In your corner since the day you were born.

Know that we love you.

No matter how tormented you might feel inside.

When you put your head on my chest.

It'll all turn to light.

Could you lie listening to my heart all day?

As I pray that you'll never leave me alone.

What would I do without you in my life?

As I comfort you with whatever sorrow you have.

Thinking I will not heal the wounds that you have.

But no matter how tormented you might feel inside.

Just put your head on my chest.

It'll all be alright.

All I can think about is you.

Just to be with you, I'd give up everything.

I don't know how to explain it.

I know the words hardly do.

They aren't even enough for me to prove to you.

You know I've always loved you.

And I always will.

For you to know the fullness of my love.

Because my love is the only thing true.

I'm willing to sacrifice.

Even though I hardly show to anyone.

That I know how to fall in love.

But if that's the only way.

To make us happy.

Only you will know.

Because the woman I love,

is you.

The voice in your beautiful eyes.

Is deeper than all Roses.

But still I'd give to you, the most beautiful girl in the world.

The one that holds my heart.

A beautiful Rose.

Not just an ordinary, single Rose.

It's my love for you from my heart.

Reassuring you, I'll love you until the end of time.

Everyday until then.

My heart will beat strong.

For all the love,I have for you.

I searched deep within my soul.

Within my fears and doubts.

And all that I've found true.

To know my feelings for you are forever.

Keep me in your heart for a while.

Even when you're doing simple things around the house.

Think of me and smile.

Hold me in your thoughts.

Take me to your dreams.

Keep the fires lit.

I'll be right next to you.

Touch me as I fall into view.

And keep me in your heart for a while.

My mind desires for a fresh start for you.

I have given you my heart.

My soul.

I wait for you.

Search for you.

Dream of you.

Now it's up to you.

To take me to the moon or heaven.

The stars decorate the sky for you.

Take me to your galaxy.

I'll accept everything.

Whatever you will offer.

I shall not disagree.

The spring displays color for you.

The rain drops desire for you.

And my blood flows in my heart for you.

I still see who you are.

Even though you're just a shadow of yourself.

I still love who you are.

And I know deep in your heart.

You know the way back home.

Just let this light of love in.

When I saw the sparkle in your eyes.

I knew that, that was a sparkle,

  I wanted to see everyday for the rest of my life.

Let the moon's glow be of emotions.

The guide of our purpose.

I'll always care for you,

 even though we're far from one another.

I miss you often.

A whole lot more each day.

Even though we're not together.

Staring at the glow of the moon.

At the stars in the night,

  I wonder.

An ocean apart from my town tonight.

As I hope you hear this cry from this heart of mine.

I feel you,

  just not in my arms a thousand miles away.

But I feel your heart,

  beating for us.

I hope you feel my love all around you.

Amidst this pain.

But I feel you in my hands,

  but you're not with me.

With all these words,

  in my heart.

I see it in the sky,

  the sun.

All of the day,

  I want to be where you are.

But there's no place too far that my love can't reach.

When I look into your eyes.

I see how much I love you.

I see forever in your eyes.

All I ever needed.

Let's make a promise.

That we'll always be together.

And our love will never die.

Heart to heart.

At times it's so confusing.

But wishes can come true.

Love is right before our eyes.

When I see our world.

Faithful, true and devoted.

I see only you.

I see it in your eyes.

You feel my heart.

It's unconditional love.

You knew it from the start.

So when I tell you, I love you.

I don't say it out of habit,

　to make conversation.

I say it to remind you.

You're the best thing that ever happened to me.

Let's stay the way we are right now.

Looking into the future.

As far as we can see.

That a lifetime will allow.

Let's make each tomorrow.

The best it can be.

There are hills and mountains between us.

An ocean apart.

All these miles that separate us.

Disappear when I dream of you.

I dream about you all the time.

Constantly thinking of you.

On my mind or in my heart.

I'm right here waiting for you.

Day after day.

And when night comes,

 it's only you and me.

Love is a gain in many ways.

But it is a severe loss in a lot of ways.

Feelings and emotions take their toll.

Causing crippling pain.

Living without one soul.

Can crumble the heart.

Loving someone takes time.

Some days the sun comes out.

And the clouds clear.

That's when you see the true connection.

True love comes alive.

Full of one true connection.

I'm your guardian Angel.

I dwell inside of your world.

I love you.

And it's forever.

I may be your sunlight,

  or moonlight.

When the night's are cold.

I'm your sheet to keep you warm.

And slip into your dreams.

Or just the wind that whispers,

  goodnight.

But forever I am your smile.

I thought that I understood the morals
   of this wide world.
I even learned the basics of how to follow
   where today is headed.
But there's a part of me, who just can't find
   a name.
To give this unpredictable emotion.
You made unclear the distinction between what's
   inside and outside my heart.
Just fix your gaze upon my everything.
Because I want to show you the kind of days
   that makes anyone jealous.
Everything from here on out will be another chance
   for love.
Our tears and dreams can't be hidden within
   a fake smile.
Until now, I've never even known the pain of losing
   something.
I'm unable to bear getting hurt, even though I don't want you
   to leave.

This feeling of being afraid to chase after you........

is a first for me.

If I just remain my beautiful self, I could finally

grow up.

I learned this mistaken idea of strength

from you.

I want to exchange sweet words with you.

Those kind of days that would surely make anyone

jealous out there.

Waiting for us!

Here I am dreaming in the sea of misery.

The trust you put under my arms is questioning my dignity

after losing you.

Have I failed in parenting?

I wasn't away for any vacation

nor was I hanging with friends.

I went to work, to make a living to pay the bills.

The moment I took my eyes off of you.

Wings of an eagle snatched you away from me.

All I've lost on the crashing waves.

I thought I was standing, but sinking.

My strength is almost gone.

How can I carry on?

Chains of yesterday surround me.

Tell me how far is north from south.

I'll come by giving myself away.

As the unheard tears of yours keeps me awake tonight.

And forever.

I love you.

Have high hopes for you.

But you left.

Without telling me why.

Taking your love.

Which kept my passions burning high.

My heart is wounded.

In silence it hides.

I still love you.

If you should ask.

I still have high hopes in which I hold on to.

I still have dreams left for us to carry on.

All isn't gone.

My bleeding heart hasn't drowned everything.

Though the pain suffocates my soul.

I wonder if my heart truly knows,

  the meaning of love at all?

I'll never forget the day we started talking.

Because that day I met my best friend.

Somebody that I need to have in my life,

 forever.

And I'll forever be grateful for that day.

Because I met you.

For all this searching you're the best thing,

 that I've found.

I don't always find the words to say.

But I think about you constantly.

Whether it's on my mind,

 or in my heart.

And it assures me that I'm never alone.

Let me hold you and vow to be yours forever.

I'll give you my love with sweet surrender.

Because I've always wanted to love you.

Our hearts will beat as one.

As I see a pure and simple honesty in your eyes,

Your smile is one of the best smiles, I've ever seen.

And it has captivated me since day one.

So let's not waste this time.

Let me fill your life with pleasure.

And make moments to treasure.

When the morning sun appears.

We'll find our way together.

We'll make it last forever.

So if you want to know how much I really love you.

Put your hand above my chest.

And feel it.

Lying in my bed as I think of you.

I wonder if you're okay.

You've touched my heart in places.

That I never even knew.

I can't believe it's you.

Can't believe it's true.

Separated by distance.

Let me take you in my arms.

Where it's easy for me to take you to the stars.

And heaven is that moment,

 I look into your eyes.

Come closer, until I no longer know where I end
 and you begin.
Put your arms around me, all I want to do is hold you
 Forever.
The thought of our bodies together.
Warm touching, moving slowly.
Kissing and whispering things.
I believe that you were sent into my life to give me something
 to fight for.
To show me there's love in this world.
To give me hope and to bring me joy.
You're proof all I need is you.
Looking into your eyes.
I'll give you my love with sweet surrender.
Because you'll forever be my always.

Take to your bed.

Where you say there's peace.

But dream of love instead.

Fate tell me it's right, is this love

at first sight?

There's more beauty in her than anyone.

As I take her by the hand.

And lead her where I will.

To make love with affection.

Give her love.

I'll sing her a love song.

With dedication and feeling.

Ones to make her wonder.

If she's feeling down, feeling low.

Let her just think of me.

Remembering she's everything I need.

And that I'm secure with her.

She inspires me to try.

But if I were to fall.

Let me fall at her door.

Because she has loving arms,

to hold me.

A thousand miles away from you.

You came into my life.

Took my breath away.

You gave me a smile.

You gave me your heart.

You gave me the feel, I've been looking for.

I feel it every time my heart beats for you.

And no one else.

The time was right for us to say.

We'd take our time.

Still knowing the road was long.

And live our lives together day by day.

We know our dreams can all come true.

We know that we'll be together.

Because our love is strong.

I'm here again.

A thousand miles away from you.

A moment in time.

Forever in love.

You're my completeness.

Everything I will ever need.

I find within your love.

With you.

All these years of searching.

I see you have been my destiny.

I'm not with you physically.

And in person.

To hold, kiss your soft lips.

Run my fingers through your hair.

Or trace the curves of your beautiful body.

But we're closer than before.

And you will always and forever,

  be in my heart.

Which is closer than anyone else.

I love you more than just words,

  to you.

This distance between us is to far apart,
  and it pains me.
I can't even smile.
What should I do when I miss you?
What should I do when I want to see you?
It's just an unsatisfactory dream,
  I'm left with.
If I only had wings……….
Understand how I feel just a bit.
Your presence in my heart.
Grows bigger and bigger, day after day.
We must always be together.
It's natural I wish for that.
I have so much I want to say.
I'm glad that I came to love you.
But what should I do when I miss you?
Simply wish to the moon and stars?

In my dreams………

You're lying next to me.

With the sound of your breath on my neck,

the warmth of your lips on my cheek,

the touch of your fingers on my skin,

and the feeling of your heart beating,

with mine.

I wonder what I did to deserve this moment?

And as you're breathing easily.

I can only think about what it is,

that I can do tomorrow.

To be better for you than I was today.

Come closer.

Until I no longer know where I end.

And you begin.

Put your arms around me.

I want to hold you forever.

In this life your love is only what matters to me.

Love which fills my life, makes my heart beat.

When I'm listening, your soft love whispers.

There is nothing more beautiful as surrendering to you.

You give me hope and bring me joy.

You're proof all I need is you.

Looking into your eyes.

I'll give you my love with sweet surrender.

Because you'll forever be my always.

You came into my empty heart.

In ways, I can't say no.

You broke down walls.

For your love to pass through.

I never resisted you in doing so.

You colored my heart red.

I never feared you.

You feel my warmth.

Let it be known.

A home of love in you, I need.

The warmth from within isn't lust alone.

But a fire of my undying affection.

Burning with hope and faith.

Not a dramatic attraction.

But one true love that my heart always keeps.

I'm just a boy with a thousand endings.

Yet she touched my heart.

My soul and spirit.

Gave me love, steady love.

I want to be with her.

Be lovers and friends.

And when we hold hands.

She'll want everyone to know,

  I'm her man.

I'll feel her pure intentions.

Two bodies.

Of where she ends and I begin.

Every night it's her I'm dreaming of.

As I keep it simple and do it right.

Even though I'm just a man with a thousand endings.

Dear heart,

There's a fire inside.

Glowing, warming.

You're a vase of love.

Of all things felt.

You're not just flesh and blood.

You bear pains.

When you forgive, you heal.

When you let go, you grow.

Yet you know that the hardest times in life,

  we go through are when we are leveling up,

  from one version of ourselves to another.

Yet you hold yourself together.

Even when you feel crushed by the world.

And know that excuses only gives someone else,

  an opportunity.

You have faith.

You're looking out the window.

Like a candle burning bright.

Love is flowing in your eyes.

A flame that burns bright everyday.

Now that I have you.

Nobody loves you, like I do.

Isn't it funny how life just falls in place?

Somehow.

Each day unfolds.

Though separated by distance.

In this instance.

I kiss the air.

Letting you know that I care.

In the wind it's carried.

Until it finds your beautiful face.

Last night I could hear you crying.

Your soul is broken.

Inside you're hiding.

When the love around you is dying.

Your heart is jaded.

You've been to hell and back.

Refusing to let it show.

It feels as if your spirit is fading.

But I'm right beside you now.

How can I make you feel okay?

How can I take the pain away?

You and I aren't an in between.

I'm tired of living, like we're just a dream.

Just because I'm not with you.

Though I want us dreaming of dreams.

Dreaming of what we think is real.

Yet I refuse to fall.

Though, I refuse to let go.

I won't let you fall tonight.

This wall around my heart.

I want to fall.

And know what true love and happiness,

   feels like.

Then you came along and busted away a chunk,

   of the wall surrounding my heart.

To only have fallen on it, to break your bones,

   against the stones on the ground.

But it's as if my heart is too dark to care.

As if my hope vanished,

   long ago.

With such rage within myself.

Locked within a cage.

Someday, I hope to face the real me.

When I face the hell within myself.

Trying to understand what's right and wrong.

Only then let's give this another try.

When you came into my life.

A thousand miles away from you.

It took my breath away.

You gave me a smile.

Gave me your heart.

You gave me the feel I've been looking for.

I feel it everytime my heart beats for you.

And no one else.

I guess the time was right for us to say.

We'd take our time and live our lives together,

 day by day.

We know our dreams can all come true.

Still we know that the road is long.

We know that we'll be together.

Because our love is strong.

I'm here again.

A moment in time.

Forever in love.

The first time I saw your face.

I thought the sun rose in your eyes.

And the moon and stars were gifts you gave.

I hear your voice in my mind.

I know your face by heart.

Heaven and earth move my soul.

Sometimes I can't find the words to define.

The way I feel about someone so fine.

At night I dream.

That you are here.

It always looks the same,

 true love always does.

Almost paradise.

Like we're knocking on heaven's door.

How could I ask for more?

When I see you smile.

When I look into your soft, beautiful eyes.

I'm reminded of what I feel for you.

Will remain strong and true.

Like red on a rose.

When your lips first smiled at me.

I was captured instantly.

The gaze in your willing eyes.

If I had to do it all over.

I'd do it all again.

If tomorrow I found one more chance to begin.

I'd love you all over again.

A once in a lifetime love.

We love like we've dreamed of.

The longer we love.

The memories just keep adding up.

The years and miles may separate you from me.

But for me your memories will never fade.

I always thought I'd be a ramblin man.

Living in the moment, never making plans.

Wondering when my heart will beat again?

Then you became the rhythm of my heart.

I don't think you understand.

You make me a better man.

The best part of me is you.

Sometimes it's hard to find the words.

To tell you how much you mean to me.

If I did anything right in my life.

It was when I gave my heart to you.

Sometimes my eyes get jealous of my heart.

Because you always remain close to my heart.

And far from my eyes.

Though we're far apart, you're not alone.

I'm there with you, you're always in my heart.

Everyday and night, my mind is filled with thoughts of you.

As long as the sun continues to shine.

You can be sure that my heart will remain yours.

I'll wait for you, I promise you.

I will.

I swear I couldn't love you more than I do,
right now.
Yet I know I will tomorrow.

ABOUT THE AUTHOR

Ernest Roberson, Sr. was born in Glenwood, Georgia, where he's lived most of his life. He is an author of speculative fiction and horror books. His 15 short stories have been published in Blood Moon Rising Magazine.